A Crabtree Branches Book

SERVING with Honor

MARINE CORPS

written by **Bernard Conaghan**

CRABTREE
Publishing Company
www.crabtreebooks.com

T0020807

School-to-Home Support for Caregivers and Teachers

This high-interest book is designed to motivate striving students with engaging topics while building fluency, vocabulary, and an interest in reading. Here are a few questions and activities to help the reader build upon his or her comprehension skills.

Before Reading:

- *What do I think this book is about?*
- *What do I know about this topic?*
- *What do I want to learn about this topic?*
- *Why am I reading this book?*

During Reading:

- *I wonder why...*
- *I'm curious to know...*
- *How is this like something I already know?*
- *What have I learned so far?*

After Reading:

- *What was the author trying to teach me?*
- *What are some details?*
- *How did the photographs and captions help me understand more?*
- *Read the book again and look for the vocabulary words.*
- *What questions do I still have?*

Extension Activities:

- *What was your favorite part of the book? Write a paragraph on it.*
- *Draw a picture of your favorite thing you learned from the book.*

Table of Contents

Mission

The United States Marine Corps is one branch of the United States Armed Forces. It is responsible for **military operations** on land to keep the U.S. safe. It is part of the Department of the Navy.

Values

Marines are expected to live by values. They are honor, courage, and commitment. These three core Marine values guide marines' actions every day, whether on or off the job.

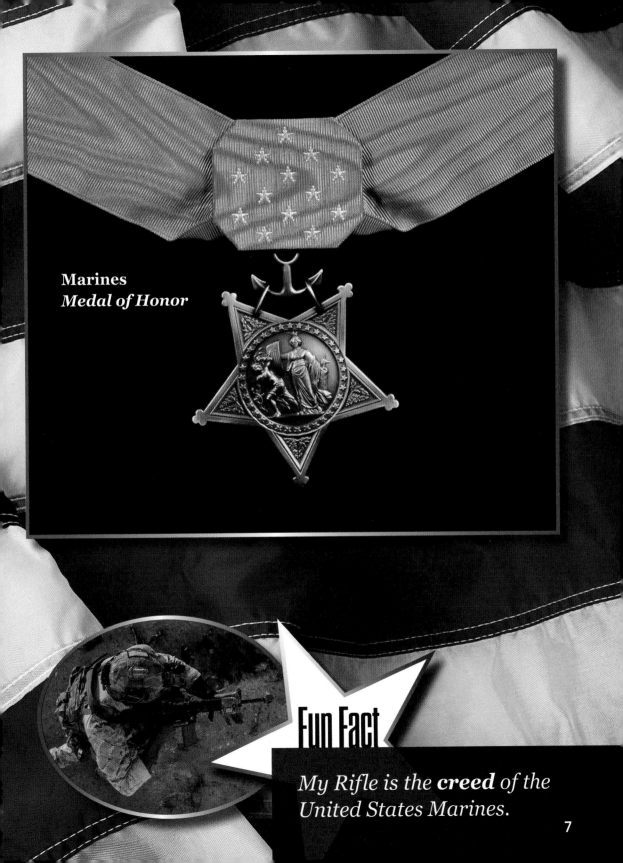

Marines
Medal of Honor

Fun Fact

*My Rifle is the **creed** of the United States Marines.*

Every service member must say the **Oath** of Enlistment. Officers say the military oath of office. This is a promise to defend the **U.S. Constitution**.

Uniform

The Marine Corps has strict rules for uniforms. Combat uniforms have **camouflage** and are easy to work in. Service uniforms have a button-up shirt. They can be worn every day. Dress or "mess" uniforms are the most formal. These are worn on special occasions.

Fun Fact

The Marine Corps Combat Utility Uniform is nicknamed "Cammies." This uniform is worn the most in a green print called "Woodlands." In the desert, marines wear tan and brown.

Equipment and Vehicles

Special vehicles and equipment are used to complete **missions** on land. The main battle tank used is the M1 Abrams. The High-Mobility Multipurpose Wheeled Vehicle (HMMWV), known as the Humvee, moves troops.

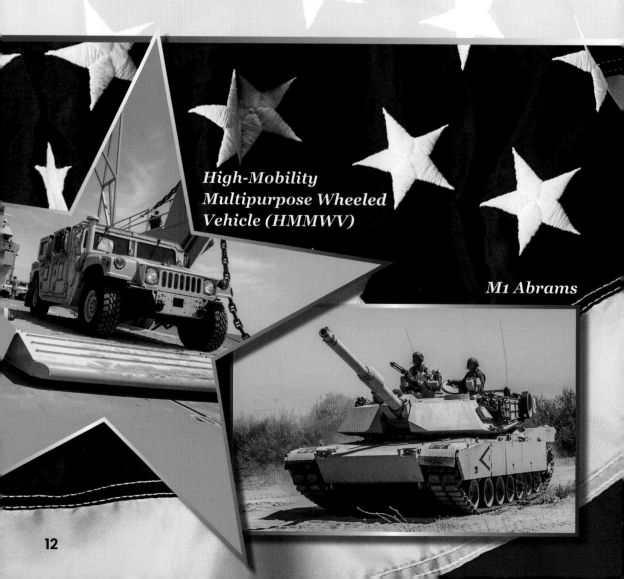

High-Mobility Multipurpose Wheeled Vehicle (HMMWV)

M1 Abrams

The Marine Corps also uses different types of aircraft. The UH-1Y Venom is a helicopter used to support missions and for rescue. Drones are used for surveillance and targeting missions.

Instant Eye Surveillance Drone

MV-22 Osprey

UH-1Y Venom

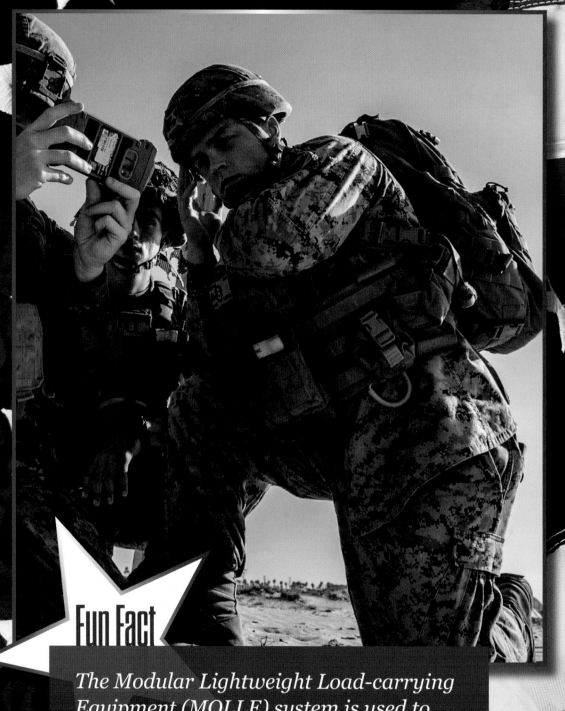

Fun Fact

The Modular Lightweight Load-carrying Equipment (MOLLE) system is used to carry gear and tools needed when going into the battlefield. It can be customized so a marine only brings what is required.

Having the right equipment is important for successful missions. Night vision goggles help marines see in the dark. **Satellites** transmit information. Laser target locators help find targets.

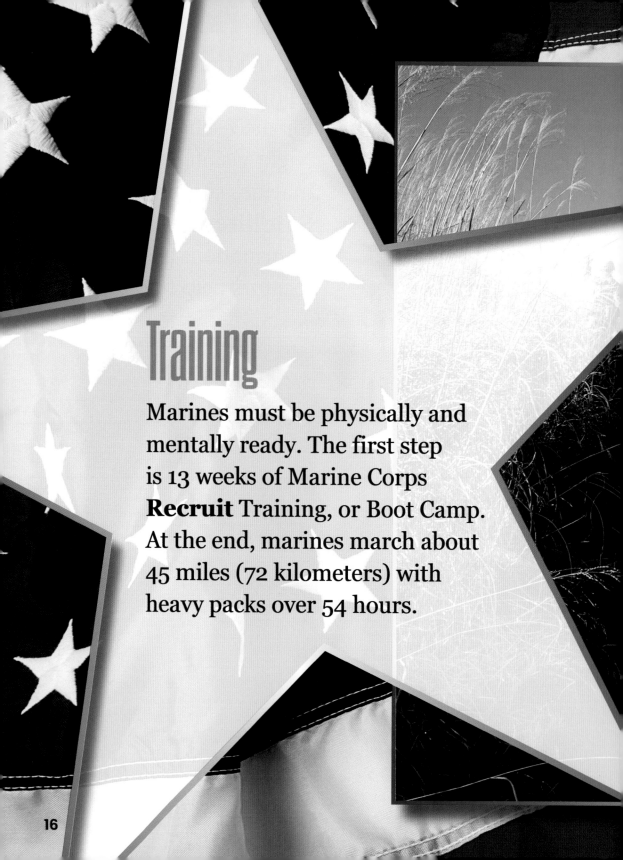

Training

Marines must be physically and mentally ready. The first step is 13 weeks of Marine Corps **Recruit** Training, or Boot Camp. At the end, marines march about 45 miles (72 kilometers) with heavy packs over 54 hours.

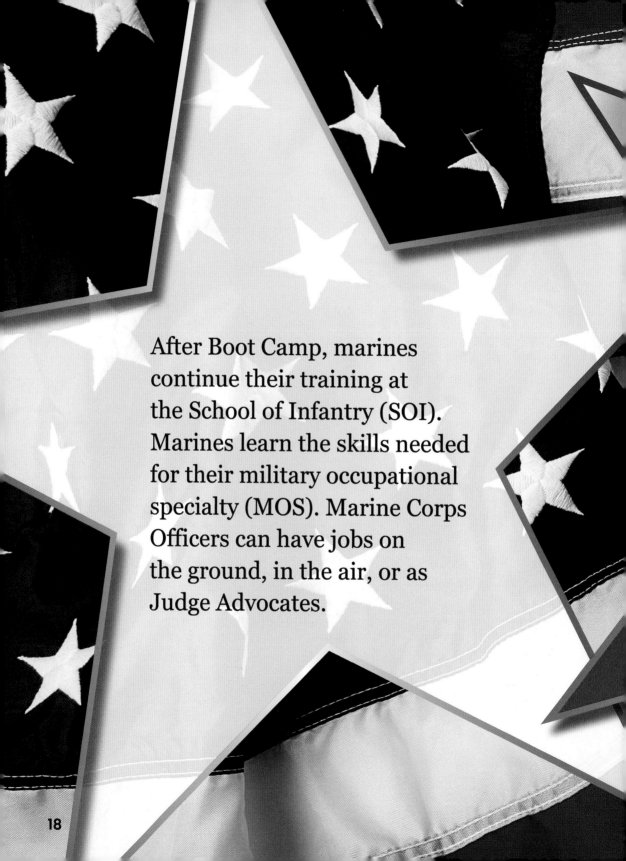

After Boot Camp, marines continue their training at the School of Infantry (SOI). Marines learn the skills needed for their military occupational specialty (MOS). Marine Corps Officers can have jobs on the ground, in the air, or as Judge Advocates.

Careers

The Marine Corps has many different types of jobs in the battlefield. Combat engineers work with explosives. Dog handlers work with specially trained dogs. Recon marines learn information about the enemy.

Fun Fact

Many jobs in the Marine Corps also prepare marines for jobs as **civilians**. Some technical training allows marines to get a professional license from trade organizations.

21

The Marine Corps also has jobs that provide support to the troops. Culinary specialists prepare and serve the food. Cargo specialists make sure that equipment, supplies, and mail arrive wherever the troops are located.

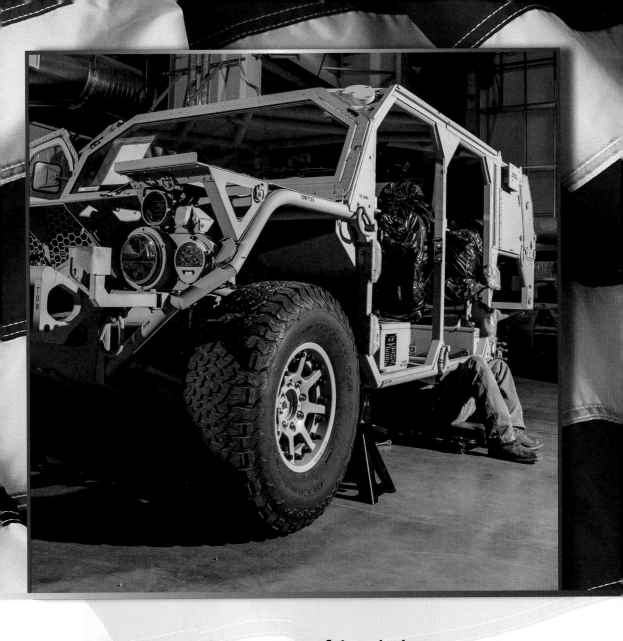

Keeping equipment working is important.
Electronics specialists repair electronics
and safely disarm explosives. Mechanics
keep vehicles running.

Ways to Serve

There are three main ways to serve in the U.S. Marine Corps. Active duty marines live and work on a base full-time. Reserve marines serve part-time and can live anywhere in the U.S. Marines can also be **enlisted** in the Army National Guard and serve part-time. They can be called by the state or federal government.

Wisconsin Army National Guard

Civilian marines and enlisted marines often work together.

Fun Fact

Civilian marines are workers for the U.S. Marine Corps who are not enlisted. Jobs include cybersecurity, medicine, office work, and support for families on base.

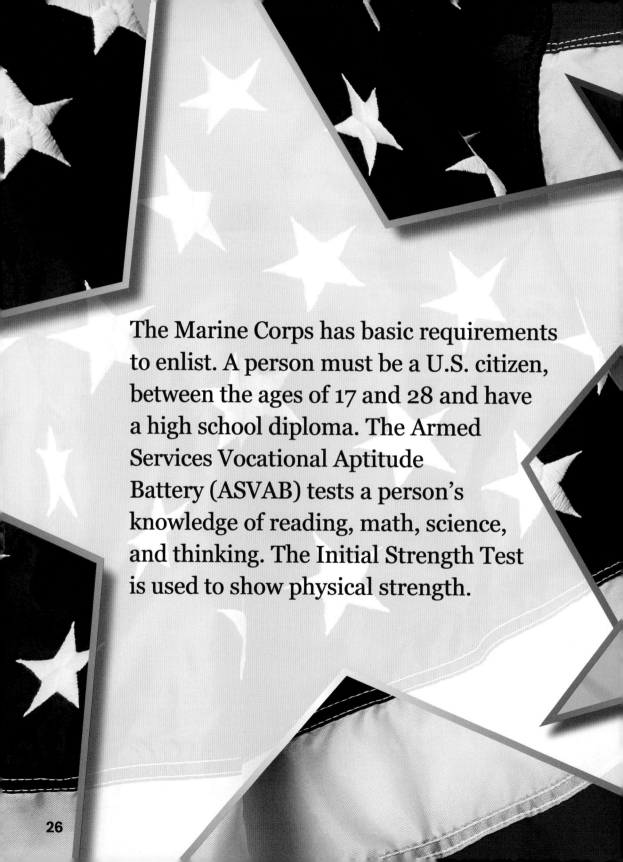

The Marine Corps has basic requirements to enlist. A person must be a U.S. citizen, between the ages of 17 and 28 and have a high school diploma. The Armed Services Vocational Aptitude Battery (ASVAB) tests a person's knowledge of reading, math, science, and thinking. The Initial Strength Test is used to show physical strength.

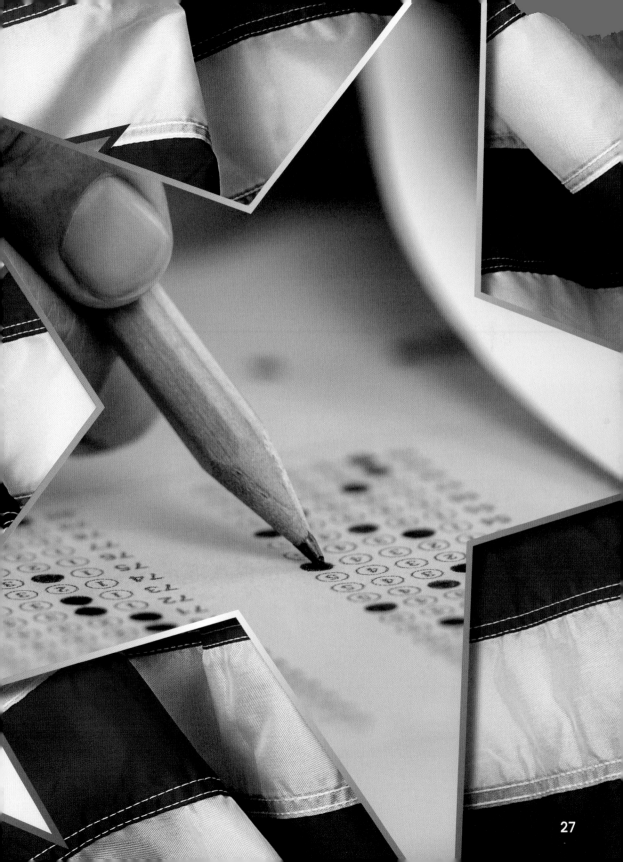

Showing Appreciation

Members of the Marines are on call every day of the year. They put their lives at risk to keep us safe. We celebrate them throughout the year. May is Military Appreciation month.

Thank You

HONORING ALL WHO SERVE

Veterans Day is a time to thank those who are serving. It is also for those who served in the past and are still living. Memorial Day is for remembering the men and women who lost their lives serving their country. Are you ready to serve in the U.S. Marine Corps?

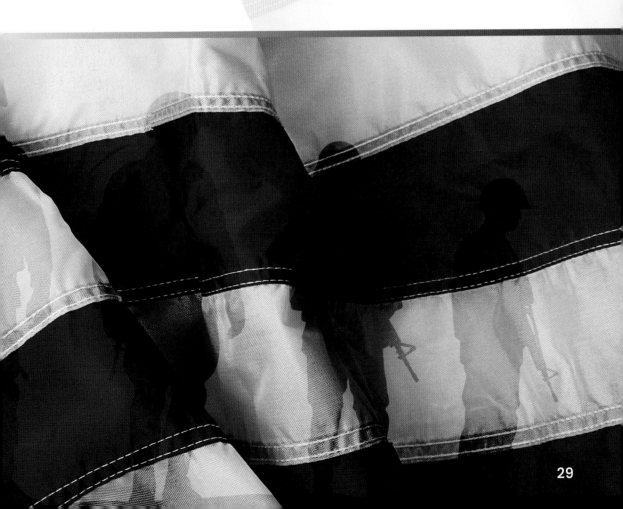

Glossary

camouflage (**ka**·muh·flaazh) Disguising items to help someone blend in with their surroundings

civilian (suh·**vi**·lyn) Someone who is not in the armed forces or police

creed (kreed) A statement of beliefs

enlisted (uhn·**list**-ed) Joined the armed forces

military operations (**mi**·luh·teh·ree aa·pr·**ay**·shnz) Armed actions in response to a situation

mission (**mi**·shn) An assignment

oath (owth) A promise

recruit (ruh·**kroot**) Enlisted in the armed forces

satellite (**sa**·tuh·lite) An item that is in Earth's orbit and communicates information

U.S. Constitution (kaan·stuh·**too**·shn) The rights and laws that are the basis of the government of the United States

Index

Websites

www.marines.mil
www.usmc-mccs.org
www.militaryonesource.mil

About the Author

Bernard Conaghan lives in South Carolina with his German shepherd named Duke. His grandmother was the jeep driver for the Major General for the U.S. Marines during World War II. He is a coach on his son's football team. He always eats one scoop of peach ice cream after dinner.

CRABTREE
Publishing Company

Written by: Bernard Conaghan
Designed by: Jen Bowers
Proofreader: Petrice Custance
Print Coordinator: Katherine Berti

Photographs: Cover U.S. Marine Corps photo/Cpl. Luke Cohen, U.S. flag ©2008 J. Helgason/Shutterstock; p.3 U.S. Marine Corps photo/Thomas Schaeffer; p.5 U.S. Marine Corps photo/Sgt. Cuong Le; p.6 U.S. Marine Corps photo/Staff Sgt. Joshua Chacon; p.7 U.S. Navy photo, U.S. Marine Corps photo/Lance Cpl. Angela Wilcox; p.9 U.S. Marine Corps photo/Ida Irby; p.10 ©2010 Keith McIntyre/Shutterstock; p.11 U.S. Marine Corps photo/Cpl. Mario Ramirez; p.12 U.S. Marine Corps photo/Lance Cpl. Scott Jenkins, U.S. Marine Corps photo/Cpl. Gabrielle Quire; p.13 U.S. Marine Corps photo/Sgt. Lucas Hopkins,U.S. Marine Corps photo/Lance Cpl. Brian Bolin Jr., U.S. Marine Corps photo/Cpl. Patrick King; p.14 U.S. Marine Corps photo/Sgt. Hailey D. Clay; p.15 U.S. Marine Corps photo/Cpl. Sarah Marshall; p.17 U.S. Marine Corps photo/Cpl. Savannah Mesimer; p.19 U.S. Marine Corps photo/Sgt. Daisha R. Ramirez; p.20 U.S. Marine Corps photo/Cpl. Isaac Cantrell; p.21 U.S. Marine Corps photo/Lance Cpl. David Intriago; p.22 U.S. Marine Corps photo/Sgt. Hailey Clay; p.23 U.S. Marine Corps photo/Sgt. Jack Adamyk; p.24 Wisconsin Department of Military Affairs photo/Larry Sommers; p.25 U.S. Marine Corps photo/Michael Ugarte; p.27 ©2019 smolaw/Shutterstock; p.28-29 Black Creator 24/Shutterstock

Library and Archives Canada Cataloguing in Publication

Available at the Library and Archives Canada

Library of Congress Cataloging-in-Publication Data

Available at the Library of Congress

Crabtree Publishing Company

www.crabtreebooks.com   1-800-387-7650

Copyright © 2023 **CRABTREE PUBLISHING COMPANY**

Published in the United States
Crabtree Publishing
347 Fifth Avenue
Suite 1402-145
New York, NY, 10016

Published in Canada
Crabtree Publishing
616 Welland Ave.
St. Catharines, ON
L2M 5V6

Printed in the U.S.A./072022/CG20220201